To Pessy

TUNING IN

Best wishes always
Kela (Rablitte)

TUNING IN

Helen Rabbitte

Matador
9 Priory Business Park,
Wistow Road, Kibworth Beauchamp,
Leicestershire. LE8 0RX
Tel: 0116 279 2299
Email: books@troubador.co.uk
Web: www.troubador.co.uk/matador
Twitter: @matadorbooks

ISBN 978 1784624 927

British Library Cataloguing in Publication Data.
A catalogue record for this book is available from the British Library.

Printed and bound by CPI Group (UK) Ltd, Croydon, CR0 4YY
Typeset by Troubador Publishing Ltd, Leicester, UK

Matador is an imprint of Troubador Publishing Ltd

To my Father,
who gave me so much encouragement over the years.

Contents

Acknowledgements

Some of the poems in this book have been published previously in the Donegal News, Verbal magazine and Beyond the Rubicon anthology by Errigal Writers.

Thanks to all my friends and family who helped me so much with this book and also to Dr James Finnegan and Paul Bradley who shared his publishing experience with me.

Transported

This place will slow me down.
I dismount and walk instead,
Drawn by light to the shore below.
In the distance I see them row
Towards the island that lies ahead.

Mesmerized by gentle sounds,
I feel the sun as I close my eyes,
Listening to water that gently slips
Over rocks, as small fish dip
In reflections of a sapphire sky.

The sound of wood on wood carries
On the water, as oars and boat connect.
Stones become fossils, back on the shore
Of Lough Corrib, where I am a child once more,
Savouring as I recollect

Afternoons spent on an island,
Playing as my aunt watches from the pier,
While men invade deeper waters
Fishing or sleeping, far from daughters,
In the same dreamland that's brought me here.

The Hidden

I was caught in a web of despair
Could not break free,
Wanting only seclusion,
To forget friends who had moved away
And plans that had fallen apart.
I had almost given up,
Like a faint winter sun
Unable to pierce the clouds.
But somehow those threads were broken
When they took me on holidays to Gyles Quay,
Where a tent became our home,
Flapping in the sea breeze,
A steady rhythm to fall asleep.
Then sitting in a church in Drogheda,
I felt a sudden calm,
Unexpected hope, a hidden presence
Like the cloudless sky we seldom see.

The Sweeper

Too much noise to hear the pigeons
As traffic passes by,
Children driven to their schools,
Who'll never know the jolly sweeper
That I knew as a child,
Who carried his brush up in the sky.

He used to tease me when I carried
My fiddle in tiny strides.
Now he's been replaced.
A machine that comes like clockwork
Even after a week of rain,
Whose noise invades from every side.

Interlude

I took you to the burn,
Crossing the last frontier,
Felt quite lost without
A trace of Eagle Field,
With slopes like wings that spread,
Now levelled, without rush or fern.

We crossed barbed wire,
Untangled brambles,
Found a path forgotten,
Marked by cattle hooves,
As you tasted honeysuckle
Entwined with briars.

My river was only a stream,
Could not compare to yours,
Deep waters of the Finn,
But at the waterfall
Down by the lock gates,
You stepped into my dreams.

Hawthorn blossoms fell,
Floating in the clear water
Where we used to swim,
When no road reached these riverbanks,
That now keep us apart
From hazelwoods and bluebells.

Unstrung

She was on the stage
Where an altar stood before,
Stainglass windows
Throwing light on the dance floor.

As she played base guitar
Her long hair swayed,
She sent ripples through
The chords she played.

She was the metronome
As I was overcome
With tears belonging to another time,
When my fiddle lay unstrung.

My hair as long as hers,
Endless empty days
When I closed my fiddle case
And lost my way.

Displaced

I find myself abroad
As I walk down Grafton Street,
Listening to foreign tunes
That gather some applause.

He plays a dancing tune,
Eyes closed to think of home.
His playing out of rhythm
With his ruin.

He cannot communicate
Though he tries to learn.
His music slips between
The barriers as he waits

In his refuge here,
His sallow skin will pale
As every soft day
Will wash his dreams away.

Out of Bounds

My aunt's bike was forgotten,
Locked away in the shed,
With basket still attached,
As she hadn't the courage anymore,
To weave between the cars,
Afraid to look ahead.

I took it to St Annes;
She warned me not to go
To the old pond in the woods,
But I could not resist,
Felt safe as I sped along
Through ancient trees and shadows.

That same bike gave me
The freedom to explore,
Till I found myself in Fairview,
Overwhelmed by traffic-
And pedalled quickly back,
To my familiar seashore.

Watching You Unpack

It's only tonight that I realise
How much I miss walks on the hills,
As I see your heavy socks and boots
Drying by the fire,
Your rucksack still half filled
With thermal vests to be unpacked.

The flask you shared lies on the floor
And when I see your walking stick,
I remember mine that I hasn't touched
A bog since June,
When I found myself neither sick
Nor well, but caught between.

I look at your map spread open,
Showing contours that will lead
To hidden loughs and glens, while I wait,
Hoping for recovery
And walks again, climbing up
Through heather, to watch the mist clear.

The Undertaker

I never could decide
If I should wave at him,
Or bless myself instead,
When he drove by in his hearse,
Eyes focused straight ahead.

I travelled with him before,
Afraid to look behind
In case we had company.
He drove as if he had,
On back roads sedately.

He played in many sessions,
Slow to take out his fiddle
As he talked to his peers,
Who played the odd slow air,
Perfected by many years.

In his own funeral home
They laid him to rest,
With his fiddle, still in tune,
Strings without notes
As his absence filled the room.

Trespass

Waiting for the ferry
To cross Brentwood Bay,
We stand on your land,
This reservation
You hope to leave someday.

There's no paint
On your front door,
Grass grows wild
As if to hide
An eyesore.

Your totem poles
Carved from trees,
Remind us of plains
Where herds of buffalo
Knew no boundary.

They have tried
To make ammends,
Gave back some land,
Built you a cabin
You'd sooner leave than mend.

Eclipsed

In the shelter, alone
By the prom in Salthill,
I hide from the wind
As waves race each other,
Without a trace of blue,
Making patterns with their foam.

A couple walk by.
As he guides her across
Rock pools below,
I think of the last time
I had someone to follow,
Under clear skies.

Unlike now, constrained
By energy ebbed,
This infinity
Of eclipsed years,
Echoes this summer
That has lost itself in rain.

The Geordie

You talk to me of Paris
Every time we meet,
How you'll get there someday,
This year or the next,
But you're drawn here instead,
To festivals you cannot miss.

I picture you in Clare
Walking to Spanish Point,
Wearing that jacket
While others swim nearby;
Combing the streets for sessions,
Recording reels and slow airs.

In workshops each day
You're content to sit,
Regardless of the weather.
At break you stand in shade
While others take the sun,
As you listen to strathspeys.

You sing in fleadhs each year,
Songs you've learnt in Gaelic,
Easier to follow
Than your native tongue,
Your way to infiltrate
The argot of our sphere.

Bray Head

We ignore the signs,
Falling Rocks Ahead,
As this is our last chance
To follow the railway line.
Dark skies clear
Above the sea at Howth.
We hear the train from Bray
As it emerges from a tunnel,
To disappear again,
A game of hide and seek,
And when it's gone,
It's only then we hear
The sound of waves against the rocks,
And I know you'll soon be gone
Exploring the outback.

We stand for a while
When we reach the last bend,
Think of the distance
That will come between us,
Thousands of miles.

Sanctuary

You despair when you look outside:
Rushes growing through the grass,
Weeds in abundance everywhere,
As though the flowerbeds longed to hide.

But it's your garden I admire:
An unexpected intermission
Between the endless concrete walls,
That have no overhanging briars.

Wild vetch compensates
For walks that I missed this summer,
Hills beyond my stamina,
Leaving me in town to contemplate.

Your buttercups bring sunlight
To a summer where clouds seldom part,
And in your trees there is sanctuary
For those who tire, mid-flight.

Last Sunset

I have no candle to burn
At sunset in Dunlewey.
It flickers at home instead,
Lit by my mother,
To mark the century
That's gone and the one ahead.

We walk past houses
Where Christmas trees and candles,
Become a ribbon of light
Across land, through mist;
As we hope for familiar stars
Through an uncertain night.

We sit together inside,
Music moves round us,
While I look through
The skylight for sunset;
No sun, only empty trees
That block my view.

I watch the grey sky
Turn to black as I think
Of Errigal outside,
But I am drawn to the fire,
To the tapping of feet,
As my fears subside.

In the Dark

How can she look so content
In her dark world, where petals
Are known by their scent
And velvet touch on her skin?

No station names
For her as she counts the stops.
She cannot see the framed
Murals that line the platform.

She can never leave
Behind the dark tunnels
As the metro weaves
Back into the light.

She does not know
Our fear in this labyrinth,
With only footprints in the snow
To guide us to the unknown.

The Harbinger

There were no footprints
From my front door,
Through the coating of snow
That fell in February,
Bringing us back
Under winter's shadow.

But I was taken outside,
When your birdsong fell
Into my fireplace.
On my chimney you found
Perfect acoustics,
For your song of grace.

You could rest anywhere,
On telegraph wires,
Or any roof or tree,
But you chose here instead,
When the house was still enough
For you to reach me.

Tuned Out

He tells me he's feeling down
On a wet windy day,
In a month when sky is seldom seen.
He's not playing with his band.
Someone else has stepped in for a while,
His only escape route gone.

He lives for sunny days
That remind him of Portugal,
Where he lived for years,
But he's chosen Donegal
To be his home,
Where one front follows another,
And on the first good day in spring
You'll always find him in the park,
Sitting beside the high wall
That blocks the north wind.

But now in this merry season
He's out of place,
As blue lights deck the trees.
Even the crib in the Market Square,
Can bring no solace
As he does not pray.

He struggles to find
His way out of the dark,
Where he has been before,
And when the fog lifts
He'll write another song,
Reach back into the void
For thoughts that can be grasped,
Like a spider's web unseen,
Until it's laced with frost.

Stepping Stone

She looks out of place in this church,
Her face lost behind a veil,
Dressed in black as if to hide,
Brave enough to step inside
A world far from her own.
There are no paintings here anymore,
No angels or saints for her to see,
A church without altars or candles to burn,
Where statues were removed or defiled
When iconoclasts swept down the isles.

As she walks between bare walls,
Does she feel at ease
In the absence of paintings,
Stations of the cross
And holy water fonts,
Safe in this austerity,
That could be a stepping stone
Between Mecca and Rome?

Different View

There's still a part of me
That wants to climb the highest hill,
Above the shores of Glendalough.
But I sit by the river instead,
Watch many tourists go by
And find tanquillity.

Pilgrims that used to come here
Over the centuries,
Stayed for a night or two.
Now people come for an afternoon,
Walk quickly across the bridge
And back again, then disappear.

I listen to a robin sing nearby,
To a bee move from flower to flower,
Watch each side of the valley
Wait its turn for the sun,
Till trees on either side
Silhouette against the sky.

I've walked little in these hills
But have dissolved into another world,
Where a ladybird explores my arm
And a robin edges close.
I've found the heartbeat of this glen
That's only felt when still.

Glimpse of Hope

Wish I could have been here
Before the war in Mostar,
Been able to walk the streets,
Admire the many minarets
Now laced with bullet holes.
Instead I feel the fear
As we pass skeletal buildings,
Like dolls houses to peer through,
With nothing left inside;
And though the shells have stopped
That rained down from the hills,
This fragile peace is not enough
To keep us here.
There are no veiled women.
Perhaps they've all gone
Or choose to be discreet.
We pass a towering cross
That penetrates the sky,
As it looks down on a city of mosques
Where prayers could not reach
Through sniper fire.

We pull into the station
Where a woman stands alone.
She smokes incessantly
Before she pays her fare,
And sits across the aisle.
As we pass a ruined bridge
That arched for centuries,
She pulls the curtain across
Though the sun's not in her eyes,
While we watch through our window
Burned out villages,
On the banks of the Neretva
And there amongst the ruins,
Lies a house that's occupied,
With new planks nailed to old
And glass back in the frames.

Exiled

We arrive in Dubrovnik, surrounded by women
Who appeal to us as we leave our coach.
A tall lady in black
More determined than the rest,
Carries our luggage and drives us back
To her small house on the hill.
She offers us coffee too strong to drink,
And in her sitting room where visitors stay,
Hangs a painting of Mostar before the war.
With little English she tells her story,
How she lived there in a city of minarets.
She says 'Too much fighting' over and over
As we watch her eyes fill with regret.
She brings us through another room.
A curtain hangs in front of a bed
Where her daughter lies along with her child.
During the night we are woken by his muffled cries.

Next morning her daughter leaves for work
Leaving her son in the shade,
Watched by her father from the terrace.
As visitors leave we watch him help
With endless laundry,
And when it's our turn to say goodbye
She gives us a lift in her Lada to the station
Where she starts all over again,
With another smile to catch the eye
Of a traveller in need of a room.

The Rainbow

They say the war began
In this tranquil place,
When Serbs took control
Of Plitvice Lakes.
Death filled the air
As hotels were set alight,
And memories of the last war
Brought Serbs to the next.
There is still sniper fire
Across the border in Bosnia,
Where lightning that forks there at night
Reflects the turbulence below.
We walk beside waterfalls
That separate turquoise lakes,
Where the only sounds
Are cascades and footsteps
On endless wooden walkways.
When a rainbow arches above a waterfall,
I remember that covenant
That was made to all,
Forgotten by those
Who live round these lakes.

Out of Range

Winter sunshine fills my room
When I open the curtains,
And see drumlins covered in white frost.
It's then I notice a butterfly
Resting on the windowsill,
Showing off its vibrant colours
That remind me of summer.
I ring you as I admire the view.
You tell me it's raining in Donegal,
But even if the sun shone,
You'd still be in your cloud
That will not lift,
Like fog trapped in a valley.
Our line breaks up and I'm relieved
As your weariness brings me down.
I'm out of range in Inniskeen,
Just as you have lost your link
To inner calm that always gave us strength.
And as I look at the admiral
Rest between the curtain folds,
I hope you can find solace
In the depths of your soul.

Out of Season

Weighed down by her long winter coat,
Orange woollen scarf and hat
That shows a glimpse of grey,
She leans on her umbrella,
Makes her way slowly across the lawn,
Eyes focused on the next bench.
She does not feel the heat
Through all those layers,
While tourists lie out on the grass.
She sits for a long time,
Looking towards Kilkenny Castle,
Maybe she was a servant there
Or lady of the house,
No matter now as she struggles to get up,
Leaving as the clock chimes.

The Welcome

Another wet day in Meknès,
I sit by the window and admire the orchids.
A veiled lady takes my order,
Invites me to look at the cake display.
She asks me the usual questions,
Her way of travelling without leaving home.

Next day I return to the café,
Content to spend the afternoon
On their terrace outside.
I'm the only one to sit in the sun,
Far from hotel swimming pools
As I drink almond juice and coffee.

And when the muezzin calls from the mosque
That towers above next door,
I marvel at the large nests
That sit by the minaret,
Where storks lie unperturbed
By each call to prayer.

When I pay the waiter for drinks
He tells me the cakes are free.
So I go back inside
To thank the owner,
And when she hears I'm leaving,
She hopes I will return, God willing.

La Chambre Bleue

Your life is full of contrasts,
Working in luxurious surrounds,
In a riad among the palace ruins
Where you serve Moroccan food,
Speaking several languages
To the sound of lute melodies.
But you've shown me another side
To this imperial city,
The narrow alleyway that leads
Across broken pavements in the medina,
To your small rooms that could fit
Into the Chambre Bleue in the Riad.
Paint peels off your bright blue walls
That match vivid cushions.
No window in your room,
Just a broken shutter in the pantry
Where children's laughter filters through.
There a kettle sits precariously
Above a gas cylinder.
I watch you make us peppermint tea,
Throw a lump of sugar in the kettle.
You drink from a chipped mug
As you count your blessings,
That you don't live in a galvanized home
On the outskirts of the city,
Sheds that would be ignored,
Only for the clothes lines that cannot be hidden,
And satellite dishes that catch the sun.

First Impressions

You walk me down side streets
To visit your family,
Though we've only just met,
As you try to reassure me
That you don't have a wife or two.

Inside each wall is tiled
With intricate patterns to mesmerize.
I follow you up the stairs
To an empty room where cushions line the walls.
You reassure me before your mother appears.

She smiles as you introduce us,
Grey hair tied back but wears no veil,
Her skin fresh to match sparkling eyes.
She has no French, only Arabic
So our conversation is curtailed.

She invites me back for couscous next day,
But it's my last night in Meknès.
She shows me her best room with silverwear,
Wants me to take a piece home,
A souvenir she declares.

I decline once more
Say that she's too generous.
I'm the first foreigner he's brought home,
So that explains how there is still
Silver on their sideboard.

Tapestry

Even though the border is closed
Between Morocco and Algeria,
They manage to get their wares across
That decorate the shop floor.
We drink peppermint tea
As the Berber men roll out a rug
And explain its abstract patterns,
This one woven by a woman
Who cannot read or write,
Whose marriage did not last.
Perhaps there are other stories
In the intricate symbols,
Too dramatic to reveal.
My sister asks, 'Did she get a fair price?'
After all her hours at the loom.
'But of course,' he smiles.
Now when I see your mat in my hall
I think of those tapestries in Marrakesh,
Vivid red against the sky,
Hanging above the market stalls
Where women sell woollen hats,
Their faces hidden behind veils,
And you who cannot cross the border
Or meet your customers,
Have found a link to us
Through the shuttle of your loom.

Travel

I meet her in the conservatoire
Where she works in Meknès.
Her brown eyes are bright and inquisitive,
No veil for her,
Instead jeans and shoulder length hair.
A student comes into the office,
She translates for him
As he has no French.
She is immersed in music,
Where sonatas slip under doors
Of classrooms along the hall.
She travels every day by train,
An hour between Fès and Meknès.
She has to live with her family,
Has never been outside Morocco,
Marvels at my freedom,
Travelling round her country on my own.
But still seems content, with more freedom
Than friends who remain in Fès.

Out of Place

Easter morning and not a church bell to be heard,
Only a call to prayer from the mosque,
No sense of holiday here,
A day like any other.
We take a taxi to the church,
Feel so out of place
As his prayer beads dangle from the mirror,
A different mantra to ours.
We drive past many minarets
Till we reach the solitary church,
Discreetly hidden behind a hedge.
Inside we hear only French,
Still feel far from home.
We sit outside under the awning
In the fragranced breeze,
As familiar words come to life,
For we've seen the olive groves here,
Shepherds who watch their flocks
And overladen mules on dirt tracks,
Bringing us closer to a story
That's rarely told here.

On the road to Tiznet

We watch the trailer in front of our coach,
Packed with girls who stand and hold on tight,
Checking their veils are still in place,
Looking away as we wave at them.
They seem relieved when we overtake.
The next trailer is full of boys
Who smile and wave at us,
Still vigorous after working in the fields.
They spend the mornings on the land
Before the heat permeates,
With no time to sit in the shade,
They go to school each afternoon
And again on Saturday.
They remind me of my schooldays -
When tattie hokers missed class,
Work now done by machines,
So different from the fields of Morocco.

Abandonment

Your guttural song soars above the rest
As you perch on the windswept gable wall.
It reminds me of the zagharit,
A song kept for a wedding day,
That I heard in Morocco,
Which led me to a procession
Of women veiled and unveiled.
They sang in raptures as they followed
The bride and groom who wheeled their cart,
Full of carpets and other gifts,
Through cobbled streets of Essaouira.
They passed whitewashed houses,
With bright blue doors,
That caught the dazzling sun,
Walked towards the threshold
With little to be carried over.
Yet all I could hear,
Was joy and abandonment
In their song, as in yours.
When you fly away in the autumn,
I hope you can return
To that same perch in spring,
And bring some joy to each cloudy day.

Fatigue

A Little dove
Flew in my heart,
My soul lit up,
I fell apart.
I grasped, I groped,
I tried to find,
The reason for
My tired mind.
I closed my eyes
And tried to see,
Why God had me
Tied to a tree.
I swung around
And felt the cold,
Then tears turned inwards
To my soul.

Refuge

She's been here since winter,
On the top floor
With seven empty beds;
Thinks of her life in England,
The reason why she left,
With no home anymore.

She goes from cup to cup
Of tea on her own,
Longs for the rain to stop,
To visit the library,
Where she can read for hours,
But can't take books home.

She looks out the window
At swallows in their nest;
Their summer home
And thinks of the winter ahead,
Of cold empty rooms,
A solitary guest.

I've seen her by the river
Throwing petals in the foam,
As she watches their journey
Towards the open sea,
Giving her courage
To face the unknown.

Soup Kitchen on Cape Breton Island

We lift containers of homemade soup,
Carry them from her car towards
The rundown hall that welcomes us,
With its Loaves and Fishes sign,
Above dilapidated doors.

Inside, baskets line the walls,
With unsold bread from bakeries,
Still fresh enough for those
Who've nowhere else to go,
Except this backstreet sanctuary.

She explains the empty seats,
Less talking while they eat alone,
As comrades cash their welfare cheques;
Walk the streets of Sydney town,
And try to forget their second home.

Persistence

She knows what colour I need,
Vibrant yellow to dispel the blues,
And every time my daffodils wilt,
She brings another bunch.
They're fresh from her garden,
Where they've been battered by hail,
While I have storms of my own.
I try to conquer negative talk,
That has kept me from my verse,
With music the only respite,
Where worries are pushed aside,
Replaced by melodies.

Slowly I acknowledge my strengths,
More vibrant than those thoughts
That try to bring me down,
Resilient like the daffodil,
Hail or shine,
That blooms in confidence.

Beyond Now

September sun reaches Salthill
With less intensity than before,
Still warm enough to lie on the sand,
To feel each grain as I banish thoughts
And let my mind go still.

But I am taken back to the strand
As I overhear some women nearby,
Talk of summer clothes packed away,
Of school uniforms being aired once more,
And cold dark evenings.

They talk of Christmas looming near,
Of shopping that will soon begin,
As if they want to accelerate
The subtle change of seasons,
And cannot wait for swallows to disappear.

Seascapes

They stand and watch motionless,
Savour each wave that falls on the shore,
Anticipate unknown rhythms,
As broken shells echo each beat
That carries across Aranmore.

They speak of their own lake back home
Far from the sea in Michigan,
With only ripples to tantalize,
Ungoverned by the sea and moon,
Locked in ice as our summer begins.

He thinks of his hut on the frozen lake,
Where he sits inside with the heater on,
Fishing the hidden waters below,
While his boat is confined near the shore,
Waiting till the last ice is gone.

They leave for America next day.
I sit on the rocks by the sea again,
Watching the waves as if for the first time,
Knowing when the tide will turn
Just as they know the thaw will end.

Song of joy and sorrow

The house martins are back again
As if to announce the summer.
But this time their song of joy
Fills me with sorrow,
As they dart around my garden.
For this May has found me down,
Unable to admire cherry blossoms
Or revel in bluebells' scent.
I try every day
To gather sustained thoughts
And let the others go,
Like the trees now so green
That had no leaves a month ago.

In my prism of sorrow
I wait for light to refract,
And reveal its spectrum of colours,
That will allow me to listen
To the house martins' song ,
And be content again.

Released

The others had just left the room
When I noticed a butterfly outside,
Trapped in a spider's web, whose wings,
Vibrant with colour, became motionless
As it hung there resigned to die.
I opened the window and pulled at the web
Shook the butterfly free once more.
It fell at first as if in a trance
Until its wings came back to life,
As it slowly began to soar.
I felt a surge of freedom too
As I watched it fly above the flowers -
Filled with hope again.

Free Travel

She asks for advice
On the forms they've sent,
Browsing through the book
Of rules for free travel,
While her birthday is imminent.

Only a month to wait
But every day too long,
Tablets before each meal,
Food that tastes the same,
With her appetite gone.

Confined to house and garden,
She carries sticks from the shed,
As she walks along the path
Through flowers and weeds,
While planes fly overhead.

She remembers holidays,
Spent hiking in the Pyrenees,
Up next to clear blue skies,
And her last flight in Autumn,
To Canada's maple trees.

She hopes for recovery,
The strength to travel again,
By bus to Donegal,
To sit by our kitchen window,
With its view of Cark mountain.

Scent of Therese

I listened to each verse as she sang your poems
That talked of joy, suffering and pain,
Was taken by surprise when unwelcome tears came,
As your reflections all became my own.
On the altar your photographs were shown,
One of you at fifteen before you gained
Entry to the Carmelites where you remained,
Till you left this world, so young, for the unknown.

I thought of myself at that age when I slipped between
Forgotton chasms, my fiddle case closed,
Smothered rhythms recalled with clarity;
Then as if to comfort me you intervened,
When all around me was the heavy scent of roses,
Stronger than incense, scent of eternity.

Leaf Trail

This is a place to contemplate,
Where two rivers unite in strength,
Carrying leaves that have lost their grip,
Some flowing on to Ardara,
Others caught in currents
Where waters pull against each other.
I know what it is to spin round,
To wonder which path to take.

Who knows which way the wind will blow,
If a leaf will fall on grass or water,
Or if something else will intervene?
I sit by faded Montbretia and blackberries,
Remembering summers before
On other banks of the Owenea;
Fears that never came to pass,
When decay made room for seeds to grow.

Birdwatch

I often heard you say
You'd like to return as a bird,
A life without boundaries.
I think of you often,
But never under the clay.

Instead I look up high,
To a skylark that soars
Above all the rest,
And I listen to its song
Wishing I could fly.

I look through your bird guide,
Wonder which you chose -
And from the cliffs on Tory
I see you once again,
As I watch a gannet dive.

And when I see wild geese
Flying in formation,
I think one could be you,
Relishing the view above the waves
In a journey that will never cease.

But maybe you're the robin
That lives in my back garden,
Who moves closer each year
When I sit outside, my door closed,
Afraid to let you in.

In the Shade

She's in the shade
Though sun tints her hair,
Turning red to bronze
Like the land she's come from,
Beams of light on heather.

She's well enough
To travel to town,
Leaving behind the desolate
Meenaroy, whose dark forest
Follows the road down.

As she waits
For the bus to come
On her familiar seat,
Groceries at her feet,
She watches everyone.

She remembers me
From many years before,
In a ward filled with flowers
Where we stood by a window for hours,
That summer we spent indoors.

She's still unwell,
Cannot break the chain,
To leave familiar surrounds
Or put an end to feeling down
And so she remains.

Beckoning

Doors have closed on winter,
On dark evenings
Too wet for stars,
On paltry street lights.
The black veil has lifted
And I can see for miles,
Follow the birds' wings.

I look towards Glen,
Watch the sun set
Above Meenaroy,
Long to stand below
That sycamore tree,
Playing in the wind,
Whispers in each breath.

Its branches frame cliffs
And frenzied waves below.
I carry the scent of roses
From summer to summer,
That grow wild near the sea,
Till I can return
Each year like the swallow.

Migration

A cold November day
As we drive along Slab Rd,
We notice brown fields
Empty after the harvest,
Now filled with a mass of white.
We stop and watch enthralled
As whooper swans gather,
Fill the air with their calls.

They pick the bleakest time
To visit each year,
With only gorse blossoms
To colour the hedgerows.
But Iceland is no haven
When winter takes hold.
So they leave darkness behind
And the arctic cold.

We get a closer look
When some wander near the fence,
And wonder how they can fly
In one day from Iceland,
To the shores of Donegal,
At altitudes so high
Their wings might freeze,
If they chose to glide.

Their necks protrude in flight
As if to defy the odds:
The sudden thunder storm
Or hunter by a lake,
Abandoned twine in fields,
Oil that sticks to wings.
They are not held back
In their eternal crossings.

Remnants

They chose a special place
Under light reflected from quartz stones,
In hills that surround the cemetery,
And glare radiating from the sea
Above Sligo Bay and Ballisodare;
A light-filled place to rest their bones.

Their fifth millennium
To lie below Knocknarea,
Boulders that still stand
In stone circles and passage tombs,
With missing pieces in nearby walls,
Adding to their mystery.

They left remnants behind,
Pieces of pottery and flint,
Clasps and pins that now lie broken,
But left us no trace of thoughts and fears
Of previous millenniums,
As we follow their footprints.

Remedy

My mother knocks on the back door
Holding a flower arrangement,
With water dripping on the path;
Her gift for a convalescent
Who's out of touch with seasons,
Blackberries and autumn scents.

It's only thrown together, she says,
But I know she's proud of her display,
Yellow chrysanthemums to replace
Last rays of early sunsets,
As shadows grow longer and empty trees
Reveal abandoned nests.

A red carnation sits among
Berries of cotoneaster,
Interspersed with St John's Wort,
That's full of secret remedies
For those who need a summer sun,
Who find winter an eternity.

Their scent entices me outside
Leaving my window view behind,
Where I've watched the end of summer,
In limited views across trees,
With energy outside that abounds
In flights of birds, in dancing leaves.